# All About Animals
# Seals

By Christina Wilsdon

Reader's Digest Young Families

# Contents

# Chapter 1
## A Seal Story

### Pup Tent

The ringed seal of the Arctic is the only seal that builds a den for its pup. The female digs up through ice and snow while she is in the water to carve out a cave. She gives birth inside this den, and the pup stays inside it for a few weeks.

**B**aby Seal rolled on the snow and ice. He sniffed, hoping to catch a scent of Mama Seal. No luck! Mama Seal was still in the water. Baby Seal felt his tummy rumble. He began to yelp and cry. Maybe if Mama Seal heard him, she would hurry back on shore!

Baby Seal's cries mixed with the yelps and whimpers of the other baby seals lying on the ice. But Mama Seal knew the special sound of her baby's voice. She could hear it clearly despite all the noise! Mama Seal swam to the edge of the ice. The claws on her front flippers dug into the ice as she hauled herself from the sea. Then she wriggled over to Baby Seal.

Baby Seal and Mama Seal touched noses. Mama Seal flopped onto her side so that Baby Seal could drink milk from her body. Then he was ready to take a nap.

Baby Seal spent most of his time sleeping or lying in the sun. The late-winter sunlight was weak, but his fur held the sun's warmth. Baby Seal was wrapped in his own built-in blanket!

## Changing Coat Colors

When a harp seal pup is born, its fur looks yellow and the pup is called a yellowcoat. After a few days, the yellow fades and the pup is called a whitecoat. In a few weeks, the white fur starts falling out and is replaced by its adult silvery coat.

Baby Seal weighed 20 pounds when he was born—about as much as three human babies. But for a baby seal, he was thin! Mama Seal's milk was rich in all the good things he needed for growing. Baby Seal quickly grew plump and round. Soon he had a thick layer of fat under his skin that helped keep him warm, just as his fur did.

Mama Seal's body was wrapped in fat and fur, too. But she lost weight as her baby grew. She could not swim far away to fish while Baby Seal was so young and helpless. Sometimes she went hungry so she could stay close to protect and feed him.

One day while Mama Seal was in the water, Baby Seal saw a huge white animal wander across the ice. Baby Seal had never seen a polar bear before, but he sensed danger. He curled up and pulled his head close to his body. Then he lay as still as a stone. His white coat helped him look like a lump of snow.

Luckily for Baby Seal, the bear wasn't hungry. It walked right by him. But Baby Seal did not pop up his head until long after the bear was gone.

## Got Milk?

Seal moms make very rich milk for their young. Nearly half of it is made of fat. That is 10 times more fat than in cow's milk! This thick, nutritious milk makes seal pups grow quickly. A baby harp seal gains 3 to 5 pounds in one day!

## Bad Hair Day!

During the time a young seal's adult fur coat grows in to replace the baby fur, the coat looks very messy. Clumps of white fur poke out between patches of the new silver fur. That's why the young seal is called a ragged-jacket.

## Learning to Swim

When a harp seal pup is big enough to go into the water to swim, the pup is called a beater. It gets this name from the way it tries to swim by beating the water with its flippers.

By the time he was two weeks old, Baby Seal weighed 70 pounds. He looked like a big, fuzzy white sausage! But Mama Seal had grown thinner. She had not eaten much since Baby Seal's birth and had lost almost 40 pounds.

Mama Seal knew that Baby Seal was old enough to survive without her until he was ready to go to sea himself. It was time for her to return to the ocean. And so one day Mama Seal slipped silently into the water and swam away.

Baby Seal waited for her to return. Many hours went by. He yelped and cried. Some of the other pups on the ice called for their mothers, too. But it was no use. The mother seals were not coming back.

Baby Seal did not go hungry after Mama Seal left. He was able to live off the thick layer of fat that he grew while drinking his mother's milk. Soon he felt a strong tug inside himself to creep down to the water. When he did, he found that the water was full of tiny shrimplike creatures. He eagerly slurped up a mouthful of them.

Baby Seal's life had changed, and soon it would change even more. He would lose his white fur and grow a new silvery coat dotted with spots. By the time he is four weeks old, Baby Seal will join a herd of harp seals whose home is the cold ocean.

**Wild Words**

*A male seal is called a **bull**. A female seal is called a **cow**. A baby seal is called a **pup**.*

# Chapter 2
# The Body of a Seal

An eared seal, like this California sea lion, can walk and even run on land! It turns its hind flippers forward and raises itself up on its front flippers to move forward—or even backward!

# At Sea and on Land

A seal is a mammal, like you, but it is shaped more like a fish! Its body is smooth and long. Its flippers can fold up close to its body. This streamlined shape helps seals swim quickly and easily through ocean waters. But unlike dolphins and whales, most seals must come ashore to mate, give birth, and molt their fur (shed old fur and grow new fur).

# Two Groups of Seals

Seals are divided into two main groups: eared seals and true seals. Eared seals have little ear flaps that can be seen on the outside of their heads. Sea lions and fur seals are eared seals. All other seals are true seals. True seals have small openings that look like holes for ears.

When a true seal moves on land, it looks much like a giant inchworm. It drags its body along the ice by pulling itself forward with its front flippers and bending and straightening its body with a mighty pumping motion. But eared seals can walk on their flippers!

**True Seal**

**Eared Seal**

# Underwater Athletes

Seals are awkward on land, but they are graceful and fast underwater. A seal's flexible body bends and twists easily as it swims. A sea lion can zip along at speeds up to 25 miles per hour for short distances—faster than a human can run.

Most of the time, seals find food close to the water's surface. They can dive about 600 feet deep and stay underwater for up to 20 minutes, then come up for air. But many kinds of seals can dive deeper and stay underwater even longer. One champion diver, the northern elephant seal, can dive nearly one mile deep (5,280 feet) and stay underwater for an hour or two without taking a breath!

A seal can go a long time without breathing because its blood holds more oxygen than yours does. It also has more blood for its size than other mammals do.

### Flip Up, Cool Down

A seal is so well protected against icy-cold ocean waters and freezing-cold air that it sometimes gets too hot. A hot seal will hold a wet flipper in the air so that the breeze will carry away extra body heat and cool off the seal.

Seals dive to amazing depths and hold their breath much longer than humans can.

## Different Strokes

A true seal swims by paddling with its hind flippers and swinging the back end of its body from side to side. An eared seal paddles with its front flippers. It moves them back and forth in long, powerful strokes.

Seals use their whiskers
to nuzzle and greet
one another.

# Seal Senses

Seals hear a little less well than you do when on land but better than you when underwater. Their good underwater hearing helps them pinpoint where fish and other food are located. It also helps them find other seals.

Many kinds of seals make sounds underwater during their breeding season. The sounds may be songs sung by males looking for mates. Scientists are now studying seals to learn if they also use sound to hunt and find their way in the dark, as dolphins and bats do.

A seal's big eyes see well both on land and in dim, murky water. The pupils in the eyes open very wide to let in every bit of light, just like a cat's eyes do.

A seal has a very good sense of smell on land. But it does not use this sense when it hunts in the sea. Its nostrils automatically close when it goes underwater to keep water out.

## Wow-ee Whiskers!

A seal's long whiskers are very sensitive. A scientist found that just one whisker from a ringed seal contained ten times as many nerves as a whisker from a land mammal! The whiskers pick up vibrations made by fish in the water.

# Chapter 3
# Kinds of Seals

Sea lions are seals. They get their name from the very thick fur around the neck of males in some kinds of seals, like these Steller sea lions. The thick fur reminded people of lions' manes.

# Sea Lions

Sea lions and fur seals are called eared seals. Their ears are small flaps on the sides of their heads. Fur seals have longer snouts than sea lions, and their coats are thicker and furrier. There are 14 kinds of eared seals. They live in many cold areas of the world, but not in the coldest parts of the Arctic and Antarctic as many other seals do.

Female California sea lions are the trained seals that perform in zoos, circuses, and aquariums. In the wild, sea lions are very playful animals. They chase after each other in the water, ride to shore on breaking waves, and toss fish back and forth in games of catch. Young ones play a game that looks like leap frog. Sea lions honk and bark loudly.

A sea lion pup stays with its mother for a year—longer than other seal pups do. It also goes into the water with its mother as it learns to swim. The mom lets her pup rest on her back.

# Fur Seals

Fur seals are named for their extra-thick fur. They have long hairs like those of all seals plus a thick mat of short hairs called underfur. A fur seal pup is born with a coat of black hairs but no underfur. It can't go in the ocean because water soaks through the hair to the pup's skin. When it's one month old, a pup starts molting its baby hair and growing a new coat of underfur and long hairs. This new waterproof coat helps keep the seal warm while it swims.

# Harp Seals

Harp seals are true seals that live in parts of the Arctic and the northern Atlantic Ocean. They eat fish, shrimp, and tiny shrimplike animals called krill. The seals are preyed on by orcas, polar bears, and sharks.

Each year, harp seals travel long distances between the places where they feed and breed. This movement is called migration. In summer, harp seals hunt far up north. They start migrating south in early fall.

By late winter, the seals have reached their breeding grounds. The females give birth on the wide fields of floating ice called pack ice. The males spend most of their time in the water, looking for females. They sing and coo underwater and blow bubbles to attract mates.

A few weeks later, the females leave their pups. They band together with other harp seals to molt their fur and grow new coats. Then they head back to northern waters to feed.

## Feather Feet

True seals, eared seals, and walruses belong to a group of mammals called pinnipeds (pronounced PIN nee peds). The word *pinniped* means "feather-foot" in Latin. It describes the winglike feet of these animals.

## True Seals

There are 19 kinds of true seals, those with ear holes in the sides of their heads. Many true seals live in frigid Arctic and Antarctic waters and on snow-filled shores.

Each year harp seals make a 6,000-mile round-trip between their feeding place and their breeding grounds. This is almost as long as an east-west trip across the United States and back again!

**A Huge Nose!**
Elephant seals are named for the male's big nose, which reminds people of an elephant's trunk.

A male elephant seal can make his nose bigger by inflating it like a balloon. The biggest noses make the loudest roars because they echo the sound the most. The biggest noses are the best warning signs to other bulls.

# Elephant Seals

The biggest seals of all are elephant seals. They are true seals. A male elephant seal can weigh up to 5,000 pounds—as much as a male Asian elephant. Some elephant seal giants weigh 8,000 pounds. That's 4 tons! Female elephant seals are much smaller. An average bull weighs as much as four or five females.

Elephant seals feed their big bodies with fish and squid. In breeding season, a thousand or more elephant seals wriggle onto a stretch of beach and lie snuggled up to one another. They look like heaps of huge logs.

A male elephant seal claims his territory on shore before the females arrive to give birth. He will mate with the females sometime later. His pups will be born the next breeding season.

Male elephant seals defend their territory against other bulls. When bulls fight, they belly up to each other and rear back. Then they lunge at each other with wide-open mouths, slashing with their teeth.

# Chapter 4
## Seal Life

Herds of seals, like these northern fur seals, gather on shore when the females are ready to give birth. Sometime after, the females mate with the males. Those pups will be born the next year.

# Herds of Seals

Seals live in herds. But a seal herd is not an organized group with a leader. It is just a very big group of seals that feed in the same area, travel together, or give birth in the same place and mate again.

Swimming with a group helps seals find food and helps protect them from predators, such as killer whales and sharks. Being with other seals means there are more eyes and ears on alert for both food and danger.

Huge herds of seals, often thousands of them, gather together on shore or on floating sea ice when it is time for the females to give birth and then mate again. This gathering place is called a rookery. Some seals, like fur seals and elephant seals, swim thousands of miles to the very same sandy or rocky beach year after year!

Females raise their pups and help them learn to swim and catch fish. How long the mom and young seal stay together depends on the kind of seal they are. A harp seal pup stays with its mom for less than two weeks, but a California sea lion pup stays for a year or more.

A rookery of sea lions, fur seals or elephant seals is a very noisy place, filled with barking and roaring. But most true seals are fairly quiet on land.

# Sea Meals

Most kinds of seals depend on eating fish to survive. But seals also eat other underwater animals, such as squid, octopus, crabs, clams, and shrimp. Sometimes seals will eat a bird, if they can catch one after it lands on the water, or another mammal.

Seals do not chew their food. They swallow it whole. If the food is too big to swallow in one gulp, the seal shakes it roughly to break it into smaller pieces.

If the food has a shell, the seal uses flat teeth in the back of its mouth to crush it before swallowing. The seal's walrus cousin sucks clams right out of their shells with its big lips and tongue!

# Awesome Appetites

A seal needs lots of food to fuel its large body and survive in cold water. A female northern fur seal may eat 5 pounds of fish each day. A big elephant seal may put away 60 pounds of fish each day—about as much food as 240 hamburgers! A walrus can gulp down 100 pounds of food a day and eat 6,000 clams in one big meal!

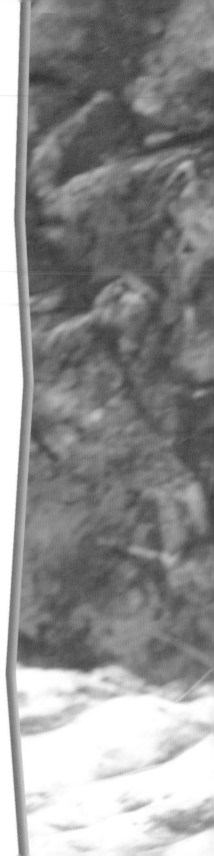

Seals have sharp teeth that are good for grabbing and holding onto slippery prey.

### Big Blubber!

All seals have a layer of fat, called blubber, under their skin. The blubber is 3 to 5 inches thick. Blubber helps these marine mammals stay afloat and keeps them warm in freezing waters.

Most people see seals in the wild when these sea creatures come on shore. Coming ashore is known as hauling out. Dozing in daylight lets seals bask in the sun's warmth.

# Sleeping Seals

Many kinds of seals sleep in the daytime because they have been feeding all night, when their prey swim closer to the water's surface.

Seals sleep on land, but they can also sleep in water. Sleeping in water means a seal must make a special effort to breathe. One way is for the seal to sleep with its head or even just its nose poking out of the water. Another way is to bob up to the surface about every 20 minutes to get a breath of air.

# Old Fur, New Fur

Seals shed their fur and grow new fur once a year—in summer or fall. This process is called molting. Usually molting takes a few weeks, but it can take a few months. For most seals, fur falls out hair by hair. A few kinds of seals lose large patches of fur. Some shed the whole top layer of skin with the fur attached.

Seals that are molting spend more time on shore. They get cold more easily in water without all their fur in place. As a result, they eat less even though they need a lot of energy to grow new hair. It's no wonder seals want to sleep!

# Chapter 5
# Seals in the World

Scientists are studying how global warming may affect seals, like this harp seal pup, and their polar environment. If polar ice melts away faster, harp seals moms will have trouble finding a place to give birth.

# Seals and People

For thousands of years, people have hunted seals for food and other necessities of life. In the Arctic, seals provided native people with everything from food to clothing. Sealskin was both warm and waterproof and was made into coats and boots. Skins were also used to make boats called kayaks. Seal blubber was burned for light and warmth. Bones were carved into hooks, knives, and other tools. Native people living at the tip of South America used sealskin as sails for canoes.

This kind of hunting did not harm the total number of seals in the world. There were always plenty of seals left to give birth to more seal pups.

About 300 years ago, hunters from different parts of the world realized they could get a lot of money by selling seals' skins and blubber. They traveled to where seals lived and killed millions of them. Some kinds of seals nearly became extinct.

## The Seal's Cousin

The walrus is the only pinniped with long tusks. A walrus chops holes in ice with its tusks to reach food. It sinks the tusks into ice to help pull itself out of the water. Male walruses show off their big tusks to threaten other males. A walrus has about 300 whiskers that help it find food underwater.

# Protecting Seals

By the early 1900s, nations realized they had to protect seals from extinction. They began to pass laws to control seal hunting. Most laws limit the number of seals that can be taken by both seal hunters and native people.

Many species of seals, like the northern elephant seal, have now recovered from the heavy hunting of the past. Scientists think there are more northern elephant seals today than in ancient times!

A few seals are still rare, such as the Hawaiian monk seal. There are only about 1,400 Hawaiian monk seals left. This seal is now completely protected by law.

## Fast Facts About Harp Seals

| | |
|---|---|
| Scientific name | *Phoca groenlandica* |
| Class | Mammalia |
| Order | Carnivora |
| Size | Up to 8 feet long |
| Weight | Up to 400 pounds |
| Life span | Up to 30 years |
| Habitat | Pack ice in the ocean |

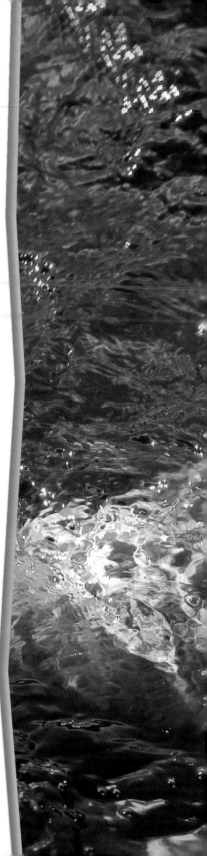

Many people are working to help protect seals and their habitats. Keeping our oceans clean and taking care of its wildlife are good for both seals and people.

# Glossary of Wild Words

**blubber**  the layer of fat under a seal's skin that helps keep the seal warm

**breeding**  mating and giving birth

**bull**  a male seal

**cow**  a female seal

**eared seal**  a seal with ear flaps, such as a sea lion or fur seal

**habitat**  the natural environment where an animal or plant lives

**haul out**  come ashore

**mammal**  an animal with a backbone and hair on its body that drinks milk from its mother when it is born

**marine**  having something to do with the sea

42

| | | | |
|---|---|---|---|
| **molt** | shed old fur while new fur grows in | **rookery** | a place where seals come ashore in large numbers to breed |
| **pinnipeds** | true seals, eared seals, and the walrus | **sea lion** | an eared seal |
| **predator** | an animal that hunts and eats other animals to survive | **species** | a group of living things that are the same in many ways |
| **prey** | animals that are hunted by other animals for food | **true seal** | a seal without ear flaps on the sides of its head |
| **pup** | a baby seal | **whitecoat** | a harp seal pup |

# Index